THE
MOST AMAZING

VIDEOS EVER!

First published in Great Britain in 2013 by Prion Books

an imprint of the
Carlton Publishing Group
20 Mortimer Street
London W1T 3JW

A CIP catalogue for this book is available
from the British Library.

ISBN 978-1-85375-908-6

Printed and bound by CPI Group (UK) Ltd, Croydon CR0 4YY

10 9 8 7 6 5 4 3 2 1

THE
MOST AMAZING
YouTube
VIDEOS EVER!

Your guide to the coolest, craziest and funniest internet clips

PRION

"YouTube is to video browsing what a Wal-Mart Supercenter is to shopping: everything is there, and all you have to do is walk in the door."

Time Magazine

INTRODUCTION

On April 23, 2005 YouTube co-founder Jawed Karim posted the first ever video on the site. It was called *Me at the Zoo* and is still there. By 2013 around 60 hours of new video were being uploaded every minute, with a billion people visiting the site every month. YouTube's 150 million videos offer amazingly diverse viewing, including corporate advertisements, vintage TV clips, sporting moments and pop videos. This selection of amazing posts mainly avoids these and concentrates instead on the site's great feature – the ability of anyone to post an interesting or entertaining video lasting a few minutes or less. So we feature the classic videos, iconic clips and great YouTube stories, such as the legendary *Charlie Bit My Finger*, *Fenton in Richmond Park*, *David After Dentist*, *Dramatic Chipmunk* and *Spiders on Drugs*, but you will also find some great contributions from lesser-known YouTubers, including Stjarnan FC's goal celebrations or the beautiful mini-films of Keith Loutit.

Hopefully there is plenty here to make you laugh, cry and stare open-mouthed, and you'll be inspired to search out more clips you love – or maybe even moved to post your own future classic!

INAPPROPRIATE LANGUAGE WARNING

The videos selected do not contain any scenes of a sexual or extremely gross nature. However, there is the occasional use of bad language which is sometimes part of the video's humour. The comments sections of many of the clips often contain unnecessarily offensive, puerile and abusive language. They rarely feature any remarks of value and are generally worth ignoring completely.

DON'T TRY THIS AT HOME

Some of the book's clips feature stunts performed either by professionals or under the supervision of professionals. Accordingly, the publishers must insist that no one attempt to re-create or re-enact any stunt or activity performed on the featured videos.

HOW TO VIEW THE CLIPS

Each entry is accompanied by a QR code, which you can scan with your iPod or iPad. Alternatively, there is a short URL address, which you can type into your own computer, tablet or phone. Unfortunately the adverts preceding the clips are unavoidable, but it's often possible to click to skip them after a few seconds.

CONTENTS

"YouTube: providing a safe home for piano-playing cats, celeb goof-ups, and overzealous lip-synchers since 2005."

Entertainment Weekly

THE
MOST AMAZING
YouTube
VIDEOS EVER!

IF HITCHCOCK HAD CAST RODENTS...

Suspense, mystery and small furry animals – all in five seconds

---

It does last just five seconds, but it has proved to be one of YouTube's greatest ever hits. Although officially called *Dramatic Chipmunk*, the rodent superstar is actually a prairie dog. The clip originally came from a Japanese television show called *Hello! Maquis Morning* in which the critter appeared in a transparent box. This would remain pretty unremarkable footage if not for the magic ingredient – three portentous chords and a rumble of thunder, taken from the soundtrack of Mel Brooks's movie *Young Frankenstein*.

http://y2u.be/a1Y73sPHKxw

THE GLOBETROTTER BOPPER

Matt dances his way round the world

Matt Harding is a great YouTube celebrity. Back in 2005, after travelling the globe, he put together a video consisting entirely of short clips of himself doing a silly dance in famous locations around the world. The video, with its infectious feel-good factor, soon racked up the hits, and Matt made more and more, including dancing underwater and in zero-gravity conditions. This 2012 effort was described by the *New York Times* as "a masterpiece" and it's hard to argue with the great moves, joyous community spirit and simply fabulous pay-off.

http://y2u.be/Pwe-pA6TaZk

A REAL BLAST

The slow-motion exploding melon

Thank heaven for the Slo Mo Guys. How else would we fill an empty few minutes, if not for Gav and Dan's entertaining and sometimes educational videos? These guys make wonderful action films from inanimate objects. On their channel you'll find a wealth of fascinating "experiments", from paint explosions and flame-throwing to a sledgehammer taking on an Xbox 360 – all in glorious HD slow motion. This one is a real favourite. They wrap rubber bands around a melon until the whole thing bursts apart, splattering everywhere like something out of a Tarantino movie. Superb.

http://y2u.be/PK8dsAeMmPk

CREATURE EATER

How animals eat their food – a demonstration

Many YouTube clips are informative and educational. Don't be taken in by the title of this clip, though. *How Animals Eat Their Food* is not one of them. It is, however, a perfect example of how a simple idea can go stupidly viral and an almost flawless lesson in how to play the straight man against all the odds. Some think this is the funniest thing since their teacher accidentally farted in class, while others are left wondering what the fuss is all about. Let's leave that to your own impeccable judgement.

http://y2u.be/qnydFmqHuVo

TURTALLY OUT-THERE

This zombie knows what he likes...

When 10-year-old Jonathan Ware set off for the Rose Festival in Portland, Oregon he had little idea he was on his way to becoming a YouTube celebrity. Even when he was approached by an enthusiastic local TV reporter as he left the face-paint booth made up as a reasonably impressive zombie, everything was normal. But with a suitable chilling stare this one interview changed everything. Within hours his TV appearance had been posted online, within days parodies and remixes began to appear and within weeks Jonathan was starring on T-shirts and ringtones. It took just three little words...

http://y2u.be/CMNry4PE93Y

PLAY IT AGAIN, KITTY

Pray silence for the legendary Keyboard Cat

A cat named Fatso tinkling the old ivories … puts you in mind of some smoky jazz joint in the 1920s doesn't it? But this Fatso is a 1980s moggie and a 21st-century phenomenon. Charles Schmidt filmed his keyboard-playing cat in 1984 on VHS only for it to find its way on to YouTube over 20 years later. From there, the cat's soundtrack was used on tons of epic fail videos with the title *Play him off, Keyboard Cat* – and Fatso became a hero. Unfortunately – Fatso never knew his fame; reportedly he went to kitty heaven in 1987.

http://y2u.be/J---aiyznGQ

TEXAS CHAINSAW HEDGE MASSACRE

The World's Strongest Redneck – living life on the hedge

One day the Darwin Awards (for idiots who protect the human gene pool by making the ultimate sacrifice of their own lives) might just feature Steve McGranahan, the self-styled World's Strongest Redneck. Steve, whose previous videos feature refrigerator wrestling, piano-smashing and lawnmower-on-a-stick, turned the stupidity dial up to 11 for this attempt to keep his privets in shape. We might say, "Don't try this at home", but judging by the state of his hedge when he's finished you'll reach that conclusion anyway!

http://y2u.be/dyWzk31p3lk

ONE SMALL STEP FOR YOUTUBE...

Gone with the Wind for the iPad generation

It takes some talent to produce a five-minute animation that reduces its viewers to tears, but the cosmic romance *Crater Face* achieves just that – well, according to the thousands of comments anyway. CalArts student Skyler Page's story is about an astronaut putting his own life in danger as he attempts to bring two moon rocks together. The video featured in Joshgi's YouTube No Cry Challenge, and many who mocked the idea of a love affair between two little boulders causing real grief had to swallow back their tears. Are you ready to take the test?

http://y2u.be/MnA4u9CaK7A

STAND OUT FROM THE CROWD

Hallelujah! At last a flash mob worth watching

YouTube has plenty of videos showcasing flash mobs: "People who assemble suddenly in a public place, perform an unusual and seemingly pointless act for a brief time, then quickly disperse" (Wikipedia). From Azerbaijan to Zambia, seemingly unconnected folk suddenly reveal themselves as all-singing, all-dancing public entertainers. Many are expensive corporate-sponsored affairs or just too downright predictable, but this Canadian effort ticks all the boxes with drama, surprise, decent singing, festive fun and befuddled onlookers. And over 100,000 likes says it's no flash in the pan.

http://y2u.be/SXh7JR9oKVE

RUN FOR YOUR LIFE!
IT'S A...?

In cyberspace everyone can hear you scream

Another of YouTube's sub-20-second "accidental" masterpieces, this has character, plot, mystery and laughs in the time it takes to butter a slice of toast. It could be the start of a scary alien invasion film or an axeman-at-large slasher flick. If it's staged this is pretty convincing, but most reckon this is from the great movie that is real life. What, you will ask, could make someone so terrified? But before you ask yourself the inevitable how, why, when and where questions, you'll be left wondering just WTF?

http://y2u.be/5JYzbzqYzm0

SKUNK ON A STICK

Because you just can't beat a simple prank...

This one's a simple and classic *Candid Camera*-style caper, which does what it says on the tin. The aim is just to surprise an unsuspecting member of the public with a furry animal on the end of a stick and see what happens. Why it's funny to see someone jump out of their skin isn't important – it just is! And the moments when the expected reaction doesn't ensue are even better. Just watch the brilliant bit with the old fella who's seen it all before.

http://y2u.be/hgQPp4nO5Aw

KING FOR A DAY

For those who like their sport with a side dish of culture

The famous Metropolitan Museum of Art in New York had just put the restored Velázquez portrait of King Philip IV of Spain on display. What better way to promote it than a signing session from the king himself? Will the public fall for the authentic-looking monarch, despite his being dead for over 400 years? Will the museum staff see the funny side? If you enjoy this creative prank you'll find YouTube has more from Improv Everywhere, a New York City-based group with an avowed aim to cause "scenes of chaos and joy in public places".

http://y2u.be/TvBbVA36y1U

MOVIE MAMMA

The Matrix retold by Mum

Sci-fi movies are pretty hard to get your head around and the 1999 multi-Oscar-winning *The Matrix* is no exception. Have you seen it? Compellingly intriguing it may be, but the plot is pretty impossible to follow. So the success of filmmaker Joe Nicolosi's mother's endearing but confused attempt to describe what happens isn't that surprising. Sci-fi nerds around the world sent this viral – but the video is charming and funny, so just who is having the last laugh?

http://y2u.be/OMf9GlLXouA

GHOSTLY TUNNEL VISION

Ghostly sightings deep in a Japanese tunnel

Pssst! Wanna see a ghost? A real one, not some blurry old
security camera image? Then click through this clip from
tunnels dug in the mountains of Japan during World War II.
The tunnels are closed to the public, but engineers were
recently sent down to test radiation levels. This film is supposedly
taken by one investigator who, after seeing this shirtless
apparition, probably hasn't gone back. The ghost itself would
scare the living daylights out of anyone, but the whisper,
in Japanese, of "I am going to kill you" would send
most of us straight back up that slide.

http://y2u.be/0dG8sfaqy1A

WATCHING THE MOVIES BY NUMBERS

100 Movies, 100 Quotes, 100 Numbers – awesome!

In response to the endless 100 Best Blah Blah lists, Alonzo Mosley FBI produced this fabulous countdown from 100 to one using only clips of movie dialogue. Guessing when and where the quotes will appear is half the fun – you know *Star Wars* and *The Wizard of Oz* will be there, but where? *The 39 Steps* (maybe you're right) and *12 Angry Men* (wrong!)? And, just like a real Top 100, he creates real tension for the Top 10. The *Guardian* was even moved to write, "This is why the internet was invented."

http://y2u.be/FExqG6LdWHU

THE SOUND OF SILENCE

A breathtaking performance – you could hear a pin drop

In 2004 the BBC was brave enough to broadcast a rare
orchestral performance of John Cage's seminal piece *4'33"*
at the Barbican Hall, led by renowned conductor Lawrence
Foster. What happens? Not much, but that's not giving it away,
because Cage's piece is three movements of complete silence.
Whatever you think of it – as a parody, a pantomime or a brutal
statement of truth about music – it's hard to deny that the
performance, augmented by the usual concert hall page-
turning and coughing, is something to behold.

http://y2u.be/zY7UK-6aaNA

A LOVE THAT DARES SPEAK ITS NAME

Does the Army really have an Arts and Craft Department?

"I've a real passion for..." It's a phrase you hear a lot these days, at beauty pageants, on politics shows and CVs, but the Rainbow Sponge Lady takes the concept and hammers it to death. She loves rainbow sponges with what can only be described as a passion. After the opening "The Army Arts and Crafts Department sent me to Korea..." the whole thing gets weirder and weirder – from "I love a sponge that is absolutely pure" to "Oh my gosh, wiggles!" and "This was one night I did not sleep." Pure over-the-top unadulterated brilliance!

http://y2u.be/ptwqeP4Feak

WEB OF LIES

Spiders on Drugs – a YouTube classic

We're used to the crazy experiments science throws up, such
as how white mice behave in a sauna or what happens when
chimps are forced to play Gran Turismo, so the idea of giving
spiders mind-altering substances on the end of a cotton bud
shouldn't come as too much of a surprise. How might these
arthropods behave under the influence of common recreational
drugs and even alcohol? The results are illuminating and
will help us understand much about how humans behave
after a joint and a couple of bottles of wine. Watch,
learn and, most of all, laugh yourself stupid!

http://youtu.be/sHzdsFiBbFc

TWO-WHEELED TERROR

From the craziest urban cycling race in the world

Extreme sports are staple YouTube fare, but now and then something comes along that gets the couch potato's adrenaline flowing. This was the 2011 edition of Valparaiso Downhill. Mountain bike riders in the Chilean town's annual challenge have to navigate narrow flights of stairs, ramps and sheer drops at breakneck speed. The course takes the riders just two-and-a-half minutes to negotiate, but each ride packs in more thrills than a whole season of Formula 1. Just watch this fella go – and LOOK OUT FOR THE DOG!!!

http://y2u.be/1ewLH0TVWkU

SPIDERMAN, SPIDERMAN...

With his bare hands, too

Vertigo warning! Best skip this one if heights aren't your thing. They certainly don't bother French climber Alain Robert. Spiderman, as he is known, has scaled more than 70 giant structures around the globe using only his bare hands and climbing shoes and eschewing safety devices. In February 2007, in front of 100,000 onlookers, Robert attempted to scale the 185m (607ft), 40-floor Abu Dhabi Investment Authority building. Even knowing he makes it to the top, this three-and-a-half-minute account is slightly terrifying – if you find it easy watching, just wait until he waves from the top.

http://y2u.be/m2TJ3tU8mbo

A RUN OF THE MILL VIDEO

Four men, eight treadmills – one big, big internet hit

Alternative rock group OK GO had already had YouTube success with a cheesy dance routine to their song "A Million Ways", but their follow-up, "Here It Goes Again", became a YouTube landmark. Not only was their next music video a chart-topping online hit, it even won a Grammy. A cheaply made, single-shot affair (although it took nearly 20 takes for the band to get it right), it sees the band performing a co-ordinated dance on a bank of treadmills. It's kind of nerdy but ingenious; great fun and altogether hypnotic.

http://y2u.be/dTAAsCNK7RA

THE BOSS OF THE BUSKERS

The streets of Copenhagen

It is July 1988 and Bruce Springsteen, at the height of his powers, is in Copenhagen with his E Street Band for one of his legendary four-hour shows. Taking some time out, the Boss goes off for a stroll in the city and comes across a street musician named John "Jo Jo" Magnusson. The busker has already drawn a small crowd, but when Bruce spots and picks up a spare guitar things get a lot more interesting and suddenly Jo Jo finds himself duetting on some classic Springsteen hits.

http://y2u.be/EQzpefkdPl0

IF YOU GO DOWN TO THE WOODS TODAY

The most chilling clip on YouTube?

YouTube is packed with people trying to freak you out with ghostly goings-on, and most can be explained by camera tricks and special effects. This video is probably no different, but there is something about its simplicity that gives you goosebumps. It's just some perfectly feasible Russian out filming his dog in the woods when he comes across something … well, something you don't tend to see every day. If you're after an explanation read the comments — or don't if you'd rather just believe.

http://y2u.be/RLqX6s39MEU

THE FABRICATED FOUR

The Beatles live on in superb Lego animation

Lego and the Beatles: both are loved all over the world, but only YouTube can bring them together to stunning effect. Using stop-motion Lego animation, YouTuber yuuhei1987 brings us the Fab Four singing "I Saw Her Standing There". John, Paul, George and Ringo are brought to incredible Lego life, the TV show set is ingeniously devised and of course the soundtrack is just perfect. Enjoy this and you'll find there are plenty of other Lego music videos available, from "Bohemian Rhapsody" to "Call Me Maybe".

http://y2u.be/_xUijgqZ-xM

PUSHING ALL THE RIGHT BUTTONS

Just another day in a quiet square in Belgium

Probably the most successful corporate-made video on YouTube, this magnificent viral ad had hit three million views in just a few days – it's now pushing 50 million. To publicize their new Belgian channel, TNT put a big red button in the middle of a quiet town square and a sign reading "Push to add drama" – and waited. Now, TNT calls itself the network that "knows drama" and as soon as an unsuspecting chap pressed the button all hell broke loose in the most exciting, thrilling and funny 90 seconds on the web.

http://y2u.be/316AzLYfAzw

YOU STUCK-UP, HALF-WITTED, SCRUFFY-LOOKING NERF HERDER!

The 100 Greatest Movie Insults of All Time

In perfect bite-sized chunks, every great celluloid curse and silver screen slur is captured. From Humphrey Bogart and Groucho Marx to *South Park*'s Eric and Ben Kingsley in *Sexy Beast*, they are packed into this ten-minute gem, venting their spleen and scorn in the most creative ways imaginable. All the greats you remember are here, as well as many that you'll have forgotten. Offensive? Occasionally. Crude? Often. Full of profanities? Oh yes! But I bet you'll be committing some to memory and firing them off yourself next time your ire is stirred.

http://y2u.be/PSEYXWmEse8

THE CUTE ANIMAL ANTIDOTE

Aaaaaaah! Look at the ickle monkey ... What? No! No!

YouTube is full of adorable creatures. Think cute kittens, cheeky chimps, daft dogs and performing parrots. It's enough to make you think the animal world is one big Hallmark birthday card. So what we really need is an animal prepared to push the boundaries of polite behaviour and ham it up for comic effect. It's a tough ask, but the good people of YouTube are always willing to please, so step forward one endearing little monkey with a party trick all of his own...

http://y2u.be/DzZqje04vLE

IS THIS GOING TO BE FOREVER?

The classic *David After Dentist* clip

The answer to eight-year-old David's question really is: yes. His two-minute post-dentist nightmare will be forever viewed as one of YouTube's greatest ever postings. David DeVore Jr had been taken to the dentist to have a tooth removed under anaesthetic. It was David's first surgery and as his mum couldn't be there, his dad decided to video tape it for her — including his son's philosophical musings on the journey home. David's father first uploaded it to Facebook, but when it hit YouTube it went mega, reputedly earning the family over $150,000.

http://y2u.be/txqiwrbYGrs

THE REAL LIFE MAJOR TOM

Astronaut sings space classic – in space!

Back in 1969 when David Bowie released the classic single, "Space Oddity", the lyrics seemed a far-off fantasy of an astronaut singing away in outer space. But in May 2013, just hours before his planned return to Earth from the International Space Station, Commander Hadfield cast himself as the song's Major Tom and picked up his guitar. As the first music video ever shot in space rocketed up the YouTube charts, picking up a million views in just 12 hours, the Commander was already fielding questions on whether he might follow it up with Bowie's "Life on Mars"?

http://y2u.be/KaOC9danxNo

THE ULTIMATE DEFENCE AGAINST WEAPONS OF MARRIAGE DESTRUCTION

**The Better Marriage Blanket –
this product will change your life**

How could a blanket help you to a better marriage? Does
it automatically prevent adultery? Enhance your sex life?
Or perhaps create a loving and harmonious relationship?
Well, this advert claims the product can do all that by absorbing
even the smelliest of farts and preventing what is often known
as a Dutch Oven. The blanket, apparently made from the same
material the United States military uses to protect against
chemical weapons, is the perfect foil to those silent
but deadly relationship-wreckers.

http://y2u.be/3yl4nErpGs8

ONE WHEELIE THRILLING RIDE

Crazy stunts from the prince of pedallers

Danny MacAskill can claim to be the first ever street trials cycling
star after this five-minute video went viral in 2009. His film was
slick, cut to the soundtrack of cool Band of Horses track
"The Funeral", and featured bike stunts most had never
witnessed before. The exhilarating film sees Danny tour
the streets of Edinburgh, riding along park fences, up trees,
down steps and jumping from one building to the next.
He soon gave up his job as a bicycle mechanic and
is now big-time in Hollywood.

http://y2u.be/Z19zFlPah-o

IS THIS THE RIGHT FLOOR FOR ... AAAAAAAAAAAAAH!

A prank ride in a nightmare lift

Are you ready for the funniest and probably best prank on the whole of YouTube? You better be sure, because this is also the scariest. It's set up by a Brazilian show hosted by top TV presenter Silvio Santos and is brilliantly simple in its execution. All they use is an office lift, a ghoulish-looking small girl holding a doll and some suitable unsuspecting "volunteers". The reaction of the terrified victims is marvellous – watch for the two women adopting the foetal position – but the stunt is so well played out that you'll feel a shiver of fear yourself.

http://y2u.be/7N5OhNpIEd4

THE WRONG GUY

The great BBC News mistaken identity story

Guy Goma, a graduate from the Congo, had turned up at BBC
Television Centre for an interview for a job in data support.
Admittedly he was a little nervous, but he bravely gave it his
best when the interviewer started asking questions he hadn't
prepped for. Hilariously, Guy had been mistaken for Guy Kewney,
editor of Newswireless.net, who had been summoned to give
his views on the Apple vs Apple court case – live on air. Watch
for yourself as Guy (Goma) handles the situation with some
aplomb. Just 20 minutes later, Goma attended his actual
job interview. He was not hired.

http://y2u.be/zWAvHnfJsOQ

SHAKE A TAIL FEATHER, BABY!

Frostie dances herself viral

YouTube can make a celebrity out of just about anybody — or anything! Take Frostie, a 22-year-old Bare-Eyed Cockatoo, who here makes her YouTube bow, dancing impressively in time, to "Shake a Tail Feather". That clip has subsequently been viewed over seven million times and Frostie and her silky moves have been back to the site, shaking her stuff to "Jailhouse Rock", "Whip My Hair", "Hold On I'm Coming" and others. There's even a video of Frostie teaching Avis, a parakeet, a few steps. Dancing animal aficionados might also want to look up *Hot Salsa Dog* or *Break Dancing Gorilla*.

http://y2u.be/0bt9xBuGWgw

YOUTUBE'S GOT TALENT

25 Things He Hates About Facebook

Julian Smith is a genuine YouTube superstar, who writes, directs and acts in his own mini masterpieces. In 2009, the then 22-year-old produced this diatribe in response to Facebook's incredibly irritating 25 Random Things About Me survey. His rant went viral and shot him to fame, but Julian was no flash in the pan and a number of other hilarious videos followed. If you like this try *Racist Coffee*, *Malk* or *Mr Timn in Candyland*. Each one racked up the hits until Julian built more than a million subscribers to his channel and over 250 million views in total.

http://y2u.be/PVA047JAQsk

SIT BACK AND ENJOY!

A brilliant set-up from the prankster master of disguise

YouTube is full of excellent pranks, but it has made the trickster's life seriously tough. It's now a real challenge to come up with a prank idea that no one has seen before, but celebrity magician Rich Ferguson seems to be a master of the art. Search on *Sneeze Head Off* for his previous stunning viral video (you could have a good guess what he does!), but before that, take a look at this ingenious tomfoolery. In order to shock the pants off people in a coffee shop, Rich disguises himself as ... well, you need to see it to believe it!

http://y2u.be/oKGerjB-d1w

HAVING A *JAWS* MOMENT

A Hawaiian fishing trip went crazy – and then viral

The day was going just perfectly for Isaac Brumaghim. He was coasting along in his kayak, enjoying a day's fishing off the coast of Hawaii, and had just begun to reel in a fine-sized tuna. But Isaac wasn't the only one out fishing that day. A huge shark also had its eyes on his catch and was about to steal the fish and scare the living crap out of the fisherman. Now everyone loves a good shark vid, but what really sent this stratospheric was Isaac's absolutely priceless reaction to the creature he later named Chompy the Shark.

http://y2u.be/puNhvXutVjQ

A CONSTANT STRUGGLE FOR SURVIVAL – YADA, YADA, YADA

Time for your close-up Mr Frog

You rarely get to see the real "behind the scenes" footage from those blockbuster wildlife documentaries. Sometimes we hear about how the cameraman spent four months in a tent in the Arctic waiting for a particular fox to walk by or the high-tech microscopic cameras that can film an ant scratching its armpit. But what about the animals? They can spend hours in make-up and rehearsals ("Could we have a little more menace in that roar, please, darling") and, as we see in this illuminating clip, face a seemingly endless wait to be called for filming...

http://y2u.be/SKRgktzRvZO

DEER, OH DEER!

The hilarious radio clip that got amplified

YouTube is so full of fantastic videos that it seems a shame to include a radio clip, but how else would you get to hear such a mind-blowing call to a phone-in show as this? After experiencing a number of deer-related accidents while driving, Donna called into her local radio station to complain about how North Dakota's deer crossing signs are causing animals to get hurt on the highway. As the internet sighed a global "doh!", Donna eventually realized she might have somehow misunderstood the situation, explaining, "In my defence, I grew up in a really small North Dakota town."

http://y2u.be/CI8UPHMzZm8

JACKO GOES STRATOSPHERIC

The original moonwalk – on stage

Michael Jackson is, of course, well represented across YouTube. Any number of his videos are available, but this particular one, in which he sings "Billie Jean" at the Motown 25th anniversary show in 1983, is of historical significance. The performance marks the first ever unveiling of Jacko's signature dance, the moonwalk (3'35" in – just listen to the audience gasp!). Those searching for his inspiration for the dance might care to use YouTube to look up Shalamar singing "*Night to Remember*" on *Top of the Pops* or the children's TV classic *H.R.Pufnstuf* episode "You Can't Have Your Cake" (2'30" in).

http://y2u.be/kXhy7ZsiR50

REACH FOR THE STARS

The original moonwalk – on the moon!

Through YouTube we get instant access to one of the most
famous TV clips ever broadcast. On July 21, 1969 astronaut
Neil Armstrong stepped on to the moon's surface, in the Sea of
Tranquility, declaring: "That's one small step for man, one giant
leap for mankind." It was one of the most amazing moments
ever witnessed on television and can still bring a flutter to
the heart – especially when you think that Apollo 11
made it to the moon using a computer a hundred times
less powerful than your mobile phone!

http://y2u.be/RMINSD7MmT4

CALL OF DUTY – FOR REAL

Helmet camera footage of Taliban firefight

Private Ted Daniels was part of a US Army team on a reconnaissance and intelligence-gathering mission in Afghanistan. When the soldiers encountered a Taliban ambush, the subsequent firefight was recorded on his helmet camera – and later uploaded to YouTube. As the squad found themselves pinned down by machine gun fire, Private Daniels ventured into the open to draw fire away from them. At this point he turns on the camera and captures two incredible minutes of frightening, adrenaline-pumping real-life warfare. Viewers will be relieved to know that, despite being hit four times, the soldier survived without serious injury.

http://y2u.be/rLHU-_OhT8g

ATTACK OF THE KILLER CARP

A family outing on a small river gets wild

Looking for a fishing trip where you don't spend hours sitting by a river wondering if there are actually any fish down there? You could try Spoon River in Illinois, USA, where the silver carp seem so keen to get caught they jump into the boat. One of those amazing freaks-of-nature videos, this clip shows a family almost under attack from flying fish. The phenomenon is explained by the silver carp being incredibly efficient at reproduction, but also super-skittish, so they literally leap in fear at the approach of a motor boat.

http://y2u.be/InENM6fwlwE

OFF THE LEASH!

Fenton becomes a dog star

Fenton the Labrador became an internet sensation and then a media celebrity when footage of him taken by a 13-year-old hit YouTube in 2012. Fenton was being taken for a walk in Richmond Park in Surrey, England, when he decided to have a little fun chasing the park's famous deer. But what really tickled the world's funny bone was the increasing panic in the voice of his owner, an architect named Max, as he hopelessly chased Fenton, while repeatedly screaming the dog's name.

http://y2u.be/3GRSbr0EYYU

GAGGA GAGGA GOO-GOO?

The most compulsive gobbledegook ever

Time for a cute one: meet Sam and Ren McEntee, twins aged just 17 months. They are barely able to stand and are a good few months away from their first real words, yet they are happy to stop for a good old chinwag and appear to understand each other's baby chat. Could it be a psychic twin thing or are the kids just mimicking their parents? Needless to say, many have attempted to translate their gurgles, but most are pretty unfunny. Go on, have a go, you could still get yourself a hit...

http://y2u.be/lih0Z2IblUQ

EH SEXY LADY!

The song that took over the world

Who would have thought a podgy, ageing rapper, unknown
outside South East Asia, would become the King of YouTube?
In 2012, Park Jae-sang, under his moniker PSY, released a
cheeky dance video to his song "Gangnam Style" and the rest,
as they say, is hysteria. By the start of 2013, the song had topped
music charts in more than 30 countries, its dance moves had
been attempted by everyone from Madonna to David Cameron
to UN Secretary General Ban Ki-moon – who hailed it as a
"force for world peace" – and it was heading for 1.5 billion
views, the highest figure ever recorded.

http://y2u.be/9bZkp7q19f0

HIP HOP HURRAH!

Fun rhyming about two-timing

A novelty rap song. Hmmm, you're probably thinking, that doesn't sound too promising. But hey, this is Emmanuel Hudson, an Atlanta-based rapper who goes by the name Kosher, and he's been going viral with a series of genuinely funny songs about life in the hood and all. "Why You Asking All Them Questions?" teams Hudson with comedian Spoken Reasons in a rap about relationship breakdown — the things she says and the chat he comes back with. It's a clever enough song, but it's the crazy facial expressions that Hudson manages to produce that really pull in the hits.

http://y2u.be/gwUX4cSwrRk

QUICK ON THE DRAW

The self-proclaimed Circle Line Champ

Without YouTube there are so many talents that would remain hidden from the world. Take teacher Alex Overwijk: if it wasn't for the global power of the web he'd still be impressing his small classes with his skill for drawing a near-perfect freehand circle 1m (3ft 3in) in diameter in less than a second and spinning them a yarn about being the "World Freehand Circle Drawing Champion". Thanks to YouTube, however, Alex's proficiency has been viewed over seven million times and now there actually is a World Championship, though Alex hasn't won yet!

http://y2u.be/eAhfZUZiwSE

EVIAN MIX THE BABY FORMULA PERFECTLY

Babies on wheels! What's not to love?

Multi-national corporate businesses with their big bucks advertising agency accounts are desperate for an online foothold. Imagine the brainstorming meeting at Evian's ad agency when they discussed their new ad. "Cute babies! Everyone loves 'em!" shouts one. "Can we have an iconic setting – maybe Central Park?" proffers another. "How about some rad stunts?" mumbles the shy, nerdy guy in the corner. But guess what? Somehow it worked. They produced a fantastic ad that has passed 60 million views and has been recognized by the *Guinness Book of Records* as the most viewed online advertisement ever.

http://y2u.be/XQcVIIWpwGs

THE MAN WHO FELL TO EARTH

Felix Baumgartner's astonishing sky dive

It was an extraordinary "event", which a record eight million people around the world watched live and open-mouthed on YouTube. On October 14, 2012, Felix Baumgartner leapt out of a helium-filled balloon 39,040m (128,100 ft) above the New Mexico desert. It took him 10 minutes to descend to Earth. Just under five of those minutes were spent in freefall and at one point he hurtled towards the ground turning at a rate of 60 revolutions per minute. This 90-second mini-documentary, including wonderful photography from the balloon, perfectly captures the story and the drama of his 1,287km/ph (800mph) world-record-breaking sky dive.

http://y2u.be/FHtvDA0W34I

THERE'S SOMETHING ABOUT MARY

A trailer for a wholly different and totally scary *Mary Poppins*

There are some pretty twisted filmmakers out there in YouTube world. Who in their right mind would take the sweetest children's film ever made and turn it into an 18-rated horror? OK, this is just a trailer, but just imagine what they would do to the whole film! It is, naturally, an incredibly funny work of genius; Julie Andrews is made to look positively demonic and the cute children look petrified. If this tickles you, then maybe you should search for *The Dark Knight Trailer Recut – Toy Story 2* or the *Sleepless in Seattle Recut*.

http://y2u.be/2T5_0AGdFic

NOTHING TO SNEEZE AT

Meet Emerson – superstar in a nappy

The battle for the cutest baby on YouTube is hard fought, but five-and-a-half-month-old Emerson has to be one of the front runners. Nearly 50 million views suggest the little chap, who looks completely terrified when his mum blows her nose, then immediately laughs hysterically when she stops, has the market pretty much sewn up, all because his mum figured out how to upload a video that day and decided to share her son's amusing moment with friends and family. Emerson, who had no say in the matter, is probably already dreading telling his school mates…

http://y2u.be/N9oxmRT2YWw

WHEN SCIENCE EXPERIMENTS GO BAD...

Coke and Mentos – an explosive combination

Mixing Coke and Mentos to produce a rocket-type blast is a classic home science experiment with added suspense provided by the unpredictable nature of the explosion. So, of course, you'll find all manner of videos recording people's adventures with their corner shop products – some more impressive than others. This is a cool one, though, that went viral because of the sheer danger of the exploding projectile. You could also check out some of the more interesting variations, from a C & M-driven rocket car to a gory human stomach explosion version.

http://y2u.be/g4kBNBEJKD8

PICK A CARD...

The self-proclaimed "best card trick in the world"

Perhaps not the best, but still pretty impressive — and, with
18 million views, it can certainly claim to be the most viewed
card trick on YouTube. The unseen magician asks the internet
to pick a card, any card, and deals out some awesome results.
It's simple and clearly executed — but there's no explanation
of how it's done. Some of the below-the-line comments
do attempt to give the trick away, but nevertheless it is
guaranteed to leave you slack-jawed.

http://y2u.be/2KrdBUFeFtY

SAW HIS POST, NOW I'M A BELIEBER

12-year-old Justin Bieber's debut video

In early 2007, Justin Bieber (then 12 years old) performed at a local singing competition. His mother posted the performance on YouTube for family and friends and continued to upload young Justin's performances as his viewers grew from hundreds to thousands. When music executive Scooter Braun discovered Bieber's vids, he was bowled over. Tracking down Justin to his Ontario home, Braun recorded him and introduced him to R&B star Usher. The high-pitched, baby-faced singer's meteoric rise made him the greatest YouTuber ever and his videos continue to be viewed by millions — although they have also garnered a record number of "thumbs-down" dislikes.

http://y2u.be/csymVmm1xTw

JACKSON IN THE JAILHOUSE

Setting the bars high

"No mere mortal can resist the evil of the thriller." So claims Vincent Price at the beginning of Michael Jackson's legendary video. Well, they may not actually be evil, but the 1,500 murderers, dealers and other criminals resident at a high security prison in the Philippines proved pretty irresistible when their dance routine hit YouTube in 2007. Over 50 million hits later, their success spawned copycat performances, flash mobs and even robot dances, and led to the prisoners taking on other songs and even erecting an audience platform in their exercise yard.

http://y2u.be/hMnk7Ih9M3o

WOOF! WOOF! … MIAOW?

Cat caught out in identity crisis

Those pussy cats can be pretty clever as well as cute. Whoever
would have guessed that the soothing purring and plaintive
wailing was all just a front? (Well, apart from the 15 million or so
people who have viewed this extraordinary and very funny clip.)
What makes it really special is the way the cat seems
to be embarrassed to be caught out. Some seem to seek a
scientific response to the phenomenon telling us, "Cats don't
know they shouldn't bark." Duh! But more agree with the
sentiment in the comments that reads, "I come and
watch this when I'm having a bad day."

http://y2u.be/aP3gzee1cps

YOUTUBE GETS MESSI

The world's best footballer in glorious, golden, illustrated animation

In 2012 Barcelona and Argentina footballer Lionel Messi was named the FIFA World Player of the Year for the fourth year in a row. To recognize possibly the greatest player the planet has ever seen, Adidas commissioned football artist Richard Swarbrick to make this amazing tribute video. Swarbrick had established his reputation with a similarly styled, stripped-down animation of Tottenham Hotspur's Gareth Bale, but Messi gets the full treatment in a gold-tinged work of art that highlights the footballing genius in all his dribbling, shooting, and even heading glory.

http://y2u.be/ma4AkKgxzxc

MAHNA MAH!

The great Muppets *Bohemian Rhapsody* cover

The first upload on the Muppets Studio Channel was *Meh!*, featuring old Statler and Waldorf discussing the Muppets' move to the internet, but it wasn't until 2010 and the arrival of *Bohemian Rhapsody* – 10 million views in two weeks – that the world realized what its favourite site had been missing. If you're looking for more, try *Ode to Joy*, *Danny Boy* or *Pöpcørn* with the Swedish Chef. Pick from the Studio Channel and you often get Statler and Waldorf's comments at the end. Although just as critical, they knock the spots off the usual below-the-line puerile nonsense!

http://y2u.be/tgbNymZ7vqY

I WANNA HOLD YOUR HAND

The Brad and Angelina of the otter world

Heavens above, aren't the human race a soppy lot? How on earth did we manage to tear ourselves away from gawping at baby animals to ever leave the savannah? This video, shot at the Vancouver Aquarium, has had nearly 20 million people exclaiming, "Awwwww! So sweet!" Before you join them, let's introduce a little scientific knowledge by pointing out that these sea otters, Nyac and Milo, are not holding hands like humans, but engaging in a natural instinct called rafting, which prevents them from floating away from each other in rough waters.

http://y2u.be/epUk3T2Kfno

A SPORTING GLANCE

A costly drop at the baseball

Sporting clips are all over YouTube and it just takes a simple search to find your favourite player, team or whatever, so we're looking for something a little different here. This clip is from a Taiwanese baseball game between the Taipei Brother Elephants and Taoyuan's Lamigo Monkeys, but the action is in the stands as a ball is hit way up into the cheap seats. However, you have to watch it out for the money shot. As the camera lingers on one spectator we – and he – catch the look on the face of his disappointed, disgusted wife sitting right next to him. Priceless.

http://y2u.be/LX-AzfLkWtY

LIVING THE DREAM

Susan Boyle's momentous first TV appearance

This is one of the most heart-warming videos on YouTube. Despite, or even *because of*, the presence of smug Simon and pompous Piers, the appearance of an unassuming 47-year-old bringing the house down still brings a lump to the throat. Susan Boyle belting out "I Dreamed a Dream" from *Les Misérables* on her 2009 *Britain's Got Talent* audition became the most-watched video of that year. It picked up 66 million views in just one week and launched the career of one of the most unlikely candidates for stardom.

http://y2u.be/RxPZh4AnWyk

QUITE LITERALLY BRILLIANT

Sing what you see

Music videos were once simple affairs – just a straightforward performance of the song. But then they got clever with little stories, vignettes of epic films or, often, hard-to-make-out and confusing nonsense. Literal versions are a genre of videos that set this to rights. It's the same video, but with the words altered to match the pictures and it's surprising just how amusing it can be. Watch this one of A-Ha's "Take on Me" and you'll get the idea. Then maybe try the literal versions of Bonnie Tyler's "Total Eclipse of the Heart" or David Bowie's "China Girl".

http://y2u.be/8HE9OQ4FnkQ

WILFUL DESTRUCTION? OH YES!

The best product demonstration ever

"Everybody knows that the iPhone can make phone calls, play movies and music, surf the web, and a lot more. But will it blend? That is the question." *Will It Blend?* videos are a series of questions asked by Blendtec founder Tom Dickson as he tests out the power of his line of blenders. Who wouldn't want to watch an iPhone ground into iDust? In his other *Will It Blend?* videos, Tom is found blitzing credit cards, marbles and Big Macs and creating a new dish, cochicken, by blending chicken and coke. Yummy!

http://y2u.be/qg1ckCkm8YI

READ MY LIPS!

The lip-syncing genius of Keenan Cahill

What's really amazing is that this teenager, miming to a chart hit in front of a mirror (OK, webcam) like millions of others since pop music began, has become a global celebrity. To be fair, Keenan Cahill is pretty good at the whole lip-sync act. His performances are understated but very comic. This video, Katy Perry's "Teenage Dream", led to his big break when Katy herself saw it and tweeted "I heart you" to Keenan. He never looked back, subsequently appearing with Katy, the *Glee* cast, 50 Cent and others.

http://y2u.be/lm_n3hg-Gbg

WHAT'S YOUR MEME?

Hold your breath, it's the *Underwater Harlem Shake*...

The *Harlem Shake* meme could have been what YouTube was invented for: it lasts just 30 seconds, is simple to shoot and edit and requires little dancing talent. The form developed from an 80s dance track, through a dull dance by Filthy Frank to a group of Australian teenagers who call themselves the Sunny Coast Skate. From there it went whoosh and within a month everyone from Norwegian Army platoons to underground miners (later sacked for breaching safety restrictions) were pointedly ignoring a single dancer for 15 seconds before suddenly finding themselves in costume and going crazy. A meme is that simple!

http://y2u.be/QkNrSpqUr-E

SCAREDY CAT

Awww! Is the poor little kitty shwocked?

Feline videos proliferate in such abundance that we could almost rename it MewTube, but this one is at least funny as well as endearing. It's even been called the cutest video in the world. This kitten is called Atilla Fluff (at this point, you need to do that "putting your fingers down your throat" mime), she's a couple of months old and her talent is ... she does a great impression of being one surprised little moggy. More cynical viewers might prefer the humour of the *Somewhat Surprised Kitty* parody video, though.

http://y2u.be/0Bmhjf0rKe8

FRUITY ENTERTAINMENT

Hey! Hey! It's annoying orange

There's this orange, right? It's got a mouth and eyes and everything (well, no arms and legs, obviously) and it lives on the kitchen table, spending its time calling out, insulting, making bad jokes and generally irritating the other fruit and vegetables. Stop. Don't flick past just yet. As irritating and childish as it seems, there's something very funny going on here and 30 million hits and a whole channel of vids don't lie. Go on, give it a go. You might find a little immaturity in a citrus fruit makes you smile.

http://y2u.be/ZN5PoW7_kdA

POTTERING ABOUT

Potter Puppet Pals prove popular

In 2006 J.K. Rowling's Harry Potter books and the film adaptations were a global success, but HP still had one more realm to conquer – the internet. Filmmaker Neil Cicierega left behind his avant-garde animations to produce simple Potter puppet plays. Well, almost. Harry, Ron, Hermione and the others were there, but they were different, and funny – as if Neil had never even read the books. It was this episode, *The Mysterious Ticking Noise*, which sent the Potter Puppet Pals series hyper, and seven years later it is still ranked as YouTube's 22nd most-viewed video.

http://y2u.be/Tx1XIm6q4r4

IF YOU LIKE IT, YOU CAN PUT A TUNE TO IT

Just how much does Debbie love cats (in song)?

Thanks to modern technology – more specifically an app called Songify – you can turn literally anything anyone ever says into a song. The Gregory Brothers have proved themselves the YouTube masters of remixes and songifications (if that's even a word). Their biggest hits are (a slightly dubious) *The Bed Intruder Song* and *Winning – a Song by Charlie Sheen*, but here they put their magic to a video that was already YouTube gold in which Debbie gets a little over emotional about her love of cats.

http://y2u.be/sP4NMoJcFd4

A TRUE CULINARY SENSATION

The song with the buttery biscuit base

Masterchef has been one of the most popular shows on our TV screens for years now, but Masterchef synesthesia took the United Kingdom's staid presenters Gregg Wallace and John Torode and turned them into some kind of dancehall sensation. Swede Mason is a true alchemist; his mash-up turns a minute's recorded foody jibberish into ambrosia. It has everything a perfect hit needs – a catchy repeated phrase, a great beat, a trippy vibe and two nodding middle-aged blokes. Bet you can't help joining in on the "wobble, wobble, wobble" bit.

http://y2u.be/IfeyUGZt8nk

HIGH NOON AT THE WATER HOLE

It's Buffalos versus Lions in the African Safari Cup

One of YouTube's most watched nature clips, this video was filmed by an amateur filmmaker in September 2004 at a watering hole in Kruger National Park, South Africa. As an almighty scrap breaks out between a pride of lions and a herd of buffalo – with an intervention by a hungry crocodile – we hear the squeals and excitement of the safari-goers who are hardly able to keep their khaki shorts dry at the sight of exotic animals attempting to rip each other apart. Whose side are you on?

http://y2u.be/LU8DDYz68kM

DANCING WITH THE STJARS

Football's goal celebration kings

Iceland might not be the obvious home of classic football videos, but via YouTube Stjarnan FC have carved out a reputation as the ruling champions – of goal celebrations. The team sit proudly in the top tier of Icelandic football, but it's these amusing cameo performances that attract the fans. Not for them the shirt-off antics or soppy hand hearts of our Premier League heroes. Stjarnan's "dances" vary from landing a fish to throwing a grenade and from ballroom dancing to riding a human bicycle. Indeed, you feel they might spend more time choreographing their moves than actually training.

http://y2u.be/ZOGByFJ-zMQ

LET ME GIVE YOU MY CARD

Introducing the ancient art of business card throwing

Although beloved in the 1980s, business cards aren't much
use for anything in these high-tec days, except maybe entering
competitions in restaurants, but this guy has found a use for his
– as a super-sharp, super-accurate, martial-arts-type missile.
If this impressive demonstration inspires you to take up a sport
that is increasingly popular (it says here), all you need is a
good supply of business cards, good hand–eye co-ordination,
a strong and supple wrist – and a complete lack of
anything useful to do with your time.

http://y2u.be/FVq0HdiM-Ok

BARK SEAT DRIVER

Meet Porter, the world's first driving dog

Now we've seen so many clips of cats looking cute, making human-type noises and, well, looking even more cute – but they can't touch their canine cousins. Dogs can lead the blind, fetch your slippers and now – those pussies are going to have to go some to beat this – there's a dog that can drive! Who knows where this will end? Traffic jams on the way to the park? Doggie chauffeurs? A Chum-sponsored F1 team? But one thing is for sure – you're going to be spending a whole lot more on car upholstery cleaning.

http://y2u.be/BWAK0J8Uhzk

"DADDY'S HOME!"

Horror recut as wholesome family entertainment

In this trailer for a nice romantic comedy, an author suffering
from writer's block takes his family to an empty hotel, where he
bonds with his lonely young son and reignites his love for his
wife. It's even got a bright, happy title: *Shining*. As you may have
guessed by now, this video does the exact opposite of *Scary Mary
Poppins* (see page 68) to Jack Nicholson's movie *The Shining*.
Don't be taken in, though, folks. *The Shining* is not actually
a feel-good movie. It is, of course, a well-known musical...

http://y2u.be/KmkVWuP_sOO

OUCH! SH**! OMG!

Knock yourself out with an "Epic Fail" compilation

"Epic Fail" is YouTubese for something going wrong. Type the words into the search box and you'll be rewarded with any number of videos full of people falling over, crashing into things, sitting on collapsing objects, being spat at by zoo animals – the kind of thing TV compilation shows love. This links to the most popular of these, which has over 50 million views – that's a whole lot of people enjoying watching other folk getting hurt or humiliated. What a sad critique of society. Still, that one where he falls off the bike is *so* funny...

http://y2u.be/Ujwod-vqyqA

SINGALONGALLAMA

The catchiest ditty on YouTube

Now what have we here? Something for the young at heart.
"Here's a llama, there's a llama, and another little
llama, fuzzy llama, funny llama – llama llama duck –
llama llama, cheesecake llama, tablet, brick, potato llama,
llama llama, mushroom llama – llama llama duck..."
Don't knock it, the video has more than 40,000 likes and
has spawned Barack Obama, Yoda and Harry Potter
versions. Now don't pretend you won't be going
back and learning the words.

http://y2u.be/HbPDKHXWILQ

SILENT WITNESS

The assassination of JFK

YouTube also serves as a source for some priceless historical footage. This clip, filmed in 1963, was not even broadcast on television until 1975. Now we have free access to the most famous 36-second film of the 20th century. Clothing company boss Abraham Zapruder took his 8mm cine camera to the Dealey Plaza to record John .F Kennedy's motorcade as it passed through Dallas. By chance, he chose one of the best vantage points possible to record the assassination of the President. Still shocking and graphic, the footage was instrumental in both supporting and disproving the conspiracy theory of a second assassin on the grassy knoll.

http://y2u.be/kMBCfxIqP-s

MATT GETS SHIRTY

A pointless but very entertaining world record

Those YouTubers love a challenge and when Matt McAllister posted his successful attempt to set the Guinness World Record for the most T-shirts worn at one time, he certainly started something. The Phoenix-based radio host had put on over 100lb in four hours by the time he slipped on his 155th T-shirt in sizes ranging from small through to 10XL, but he'd got his name in the famous book. His record was short-lived though, with many others taking him on. The latest record stands at 247 and is there on YouTube, but Matt's attempt remains the original and by far the best fun.

http://y2u.be/r6tlw-oPDBM

STREETS OF SAN FRANCISCO

A high-octane stunt ride in the heart of the city

It's a tyre-shredding, donut-pulling, jump-drift-driving feast on the streets of San Francisco as rally driver Ken Block takes his Ford Fiesta (not like yours, no) round the city like he's running very late for an important appointment. This is top stunt driving with Ken taking sharp curves at 160km/ph (100mph), spinning round cable cars and going airborne over San Francisco's famous city hills. Fortunately the city seems eerily desolate, so Ken doesn't have to worry about encountering any grannies on zebra crossings or getting stuck behind an ice cream van.

http://y2u.be/LuDN2bClyus

MURDER BY DEATH

The Top 10 hilarious movie murders

You'll find Top 10s of just about everything, but this one is quite special. Have you got a favourite movie death? Well, it's probably not in this list. They are not all obscure B-movie fatalities, but they are all gross, violent or just very, very funny. Who couldn't love the self-combusting-out-of-pure-anger bodyguard or not find the murder by frisbee strangely compelling? The only criticism? Check out the extraordinary *Worst Movie Death Scene Ever* clip. Surely that should be on this list, too?

http://y2u.be/be7nHzijyGE

GRIN AND BEAR IT

Man versus bear in one of the best commercials ever

The John West Salmon Bear Fight has been named the funniest advert of all time. Yes, you may have seen it already, but it's always worth another viewing. The ad begins as a nature documentary about bears fishing for salmon. Then a screaming fisherman suddenly runs into the scene, determined to fight the bears for the best fish. Despite the bears' natural fighting ability and dazzling kung fu moves, the fisherman has a couple of dirty tricks up his sleeve.

http://y2u.be/CVS1UfCfxlU

BEST BY A LONG CHALK

The amazing 3D pavement artist

There are some things you wouldn't believe if you didn't see them taking shape before your eyes. If the most you ever learned in art was how to make trees look like they're far away by drawing them very small, you'll be amazed by the talent of artist Chris Carlson. With just a set square, a ruler and some chalk, he draws a brilliant three-dimensional Super Mario vaulting over a game controller – on the pavement! The 11 hours of intense labour are reduced to four mesmerizing, time-lapsed minutes as his masterpiece takes shape.

http://y2u.be/U2juYr2Xjeo

BACK TO THE DRAWING BOARD

The King of YouTube draws his life

Ryan Higa is pretty much the biggest YouTube celebrity around. He has nearly eight million subscribers to the short comedy films and sketches on his channel. So when Ryan joined the Draw my Life fad that was sweeping YouTube, folk sat up and took notice. The meme involves YouTubers' autobiographies accompanied by their drawings of stick men. Yes, OK, but Ryan is a consummate artist and his story, from birth to present, is brilliantly told, wonderfully drawn and totally, totally inspiring.

http://y2u.be/KPmoDYayoLE

LABOUR OF LOVE

A portrait of a pregnancy

Time-lapse portraits are often an interesting way to waste your time on YouTube. The fascinating *She Takes a Photo Every Day*, which covers five years in just a minute, is one such project. This time-lapse story of a pregnancy condensing nine months into 90 seconds is even better. Taking a picture in the same pose throughout, it documents the growth of the expectant mother's bump and the subtle ways in which life changes around her. It's incredibly sweet, has a nice sense of humour and has a great and creative ending – in every sense of the word.

http://y2u.be/nKnfjdEPLJ0

JUST KIDDING!

The cruellest prank ever?

There are some things in life you just can't do. Like giving the opposition a penalty at Old Trafford, telling Eamonn Holmes he's carrying an extra pound or two or asking Prince Charles if he'll ever be king. Telling your kids you've eaten their hard-earned Halloween sweets is in the same league — so expect the worst to happen. US chat show host Jimmy Kimmell asked his viewers to do just that and film the little treasures' reactions. The result? A fabulous montage of spoiled brats, sugar-addicted toddlers and a couple of sweethearts that make you instantly forgive all the rest!

A WORLD AT HIS FINGERTIPS

A beautifully woven holographic love story

Imagine you could create a city for the one you love, with streets, houses and buildings loaded with meaning. What would it look like? Paris? Venice? Harlow New Town? World Builder, a captivating ten-minute story by Hollywood special effects man Bruce Banit, explores just such an idea. It starts with a guy in an empty space and follows him as he constructs a perfect world around him using holographic tools. It's engrossing, hauntingly beautiful and emotionally charged. By the closing credits you might even be shedding a tear.

http://y2u.be/VzFpg271sm8

IT'S A BEAUTIFUL WORLD

Films that make our world look like toytown

If you're told that Keith Loutit, the genius behind this three-minute jewel of a film, uses tilt-shift photography to achieve his unique filmed style, would you be any the wiser? Enough to say that the fabulous, real but miniature, world he creates is bewitching. Colours are brilliant, movement is jerky and everyone and everything looks like they are in some kind of wonderland. Bathtub (this is Bathtub IV) is actually Sydney and in his other films Keith shows he can also give London, Singapore and other destinations a similarly enchanting veneer.

http://y2u.be/LkrtYRxGyuo

CAN YOU KICK IT?

When breakdancing goes bad

Streetdance and breakdancing are popular YouTube genres and so are cute little toddlers, so just imagine what a viral hit you get if you combine them. Of course you could search for "Tiny kid break dancing" and watch six-year-old Jaylen bustin' his moves on American TV, but this is much, much more fun. This ad hoc Times Square show is smooth and well-rehearsed. Now just watch this kid go. He throws some tricky moves... That could be a helicopter, that's maybe something like a double pencil drop followed by a suicide corkscrew and here comes the best bit... They call it the streetfighter!

http://y2u.be/NqS9N7WJOFY

AMAZING BOUNCING BEAR

A tranquilizer dart, a trampoline and a falling bear...

Some American towns have a real problem with hungry bears encroaching into urban areas. They leave their rubbish everywhere, take up valuable room on public transport and deliver quite a shock when leaping out of trees. So, as this video illustrates, US authorities are empowered to humiliate them and send the disgraced creatures back home to tell their pals of their unfortunate experiences in the big city. We're waiting for the video of the one made to perform on *America's Got Talent*, but in the meantime we can make do with this shameful exercise.

http://y2u.be/Pa1pI04_IUY

THE GUILTY PARTY BOY

Australian teenager who became an internet hero

Corey Worthington – what a guy! Millions of teenagers around the world tipped a baseball cap to the 16-year-old Aussie who put on a party to end all parties – and refused to grovel in apology. With his parents on holiday, Corey threw a party, advertised it on social networks and seemed delighted that a few hundred turned up, trashed the place and his neighbours' cars, and fought with police. Watch Corey make mincemeat of the haughty news presenter – and never, but never, ask him to take off his shades!

http://y2u.be/xc0CB6URrV0

IT'S A SHEEP SHOT, BUT IT WORKS!

A viral victory for sheep choreography

As tantalizing as the title *Extreme Sheep LED Art* is, what this Samsung-sponsored video delivers is altogether more gobsmacking. It's a version of *One Man and His Dog* if said man wasn't a Welsh farmer in a flat cap but a groovy artist type with a crazy haircut. Putting a flock of sheep in light-studded jackets and herding them into well-rehearsed shapes around the Brecon Beacons produces the most incredible results. Not to give anything away, but it's not often you come away from a farm thinking the Pong was fantastic...

http://y2u.be/D2FX9rviEhw

LET'S TWIST AGAIN

Team Hot Wheels pulls off a record-breaking stunt

Remember Hot Wheels, the kids' toy cars that performed stunts on bright orange tracks? Well, they have produced real-life daredevil vids as full-scale versions of their cars (on orange tracks!) break all kinds of stunt records. Elsewhere you can find double loops and the longest jump in a four-wheeled vehicle, but this corkscrew jump, first performed in the James Bond movie *The Man with the Golden Gun*, is the most fun. Hollywood stunt man Brent Fletcher uses a split-level ramp to spin his souped-up buggy through the air at a rate of 230 degrees per second for 28m (92ft).

http://y2u.be/s48hfG0bi_l

KITTENS, FIREMEN, TEQUILA

Could a kitten-saving fireman save your evening?

Make It with a Fireman – this must be one for the ladies and this Tequila company goes straight for a knock-out blow. "What do women like?" they've asked themselves. "Why, men in uniform, kittens, a sense of humour and a strong margarita," they've answered. "Being a fireman is more than putting out blazes and giving kittens CPR," says the hunky, stripped-to-the-waist fireman. "Sometimes my duty demands I fan the flames." Patronizing, a little sexist and ridiculously old-fashioned it may be, but it's very funny and it's pulling in the views. Maybe it's that cute kitten?

http://y2u.be/cwWnlhFd8gA

THE ICE-DUDE COMETH

German attempts cannonball into frozen pool

Should there ever be a YouTube dictionary, this would have to be the illustration for the entry on *Schadenfreude* (taking pleasure from the misfortunes of others), especially as it, too, is of German origin. Although just a short video of a man jumping into a pool, this really is the perfect clip. It is concise, hilarious and looks horribly painful (without being gory or tragic). You may lack sympathy for our freezing hero in swimming briefs as he indulges in some full-blown machismo and totally arrogant posturing, but the almost inevitable slapstick, his reaction and the contagious hysterics bestow instant forgiveness.

http://y2u.be/VBXKoZQwvDE

THE MOST FAMOUS SNEEZE ON THE PLANET

A panda and her cub go viral

How many views does a clip need before it becomes a YouTube cliché? This one has had over 150 million and must be the most watched 17 seconds on the site. Mao Mao and her cub have been parodied everywhere, had a mention on *South Park* and have even inspired a video game. If you haven't seen it, watch it now — it's worth 17 seconds of your time, promise. If you have seen it, watch it again. Some people have been known to sit all day (usually at work) watching it over and over.

http://y2u.be/FzRH3iTQPrk

INTO THE LION'S DEN

The incredible story of Christian the Lion

In 1969 John Rendall and Ace Berg saw a lion cub for sale in Harrods. They named him Christian and took him back to their London flat. Within a year Christian had grown to an unmanageable size and they were forced to arrange his re-introduction to the wild in Africa. Another year passed and his former owners headed out to Kenya to find him. By then, Christian had a new life and his own pride and, so they were told, would never remember them. This video shows just what happened — and remains one of the most heart-warming videos on YouTube.

http://y2u.be/btuxO-C2IzE

GUIDE TO BATHROOM ETTI-CAT!

He's a cat flushing the toilet

Let's face it. You could upload a 50-second clip of a cat doing virtually anything and earn thousands of YouTube hits in days. So, credit to dragonzice1 for bothering to edit together a series of cats who are clever enough to have mastered pulling the flush in the toilet (a feat many human men have still to master on a regular basis). Even better, there's a rather catchy ditty to accompany the footage of these masterful moggies... Altogether now, "He's a cat – miaow – flushing the toilet – he's a cat..."

http://y2u.be/saQcnblLinc

CAN YOU FEEL THE FORCE?

A mini Darth Vader in the best advert ever

The most shared ad of all time, this was Volkswagen's effort for
America's 2011 Superbowl break, the Valhalla of TV advertising.
"Leaked" on to YouTube a week previously, the commercial had
already notched ten million views by the time it was broadcast.
It took just a little bit of *Star Wars*, a healthy dollop of cute kid
and a shiny new car to make a 60-second advertising legend.
The tale was, however, made more poignant when it was revealed
that the ad's seven-year-old star, Max Page, had a congenital
heart defect and was facing open-heart surgery.

http://y2u.be/R55e-uHQna0

THE ULTIMATE NUMBERS GAME

Countdown's most awesome moment

This clip has been taken from the golden era of the British daytime word and numbers TV game show when it was still hosted by the ever-genial late Richard Whitely and his boffin bombshell assistant Carol Vorderman. The numbers game is a popular part of the show as contestants are given 30 seconds to reach a randomly chosen target total from six pre-selected numbers. Such was Carol's mental maths genius that she could nearly always match the contestants. Then this episode came along... Too clever-clever for you? OK, Philistines, you can search on *Countdown* blooper for clips of rude words making an inadvertent appearance!

http://y2u.be/pfa3MHLLSWI

ROLLING IN THE AISLE

That famous Royal Wedding spoof

In April 2011, as Royal fever hit Britain in anticipation of the wedding of Prince William and Kate Middleton, T-Mobile grasped the opportunity to make a splash with their own version of the wedding entrance. Obviously fearing an "off with their heads" reaction, T-Mobile hung on the right side of tasteful, as various royal lookalikes and a fake archbishop bumped and ground their way down the aisle to an East 17 track. The ad was a viral sensation. Justin Bieber tweeted his enthusiasm to his nine million followers and Prince Harry apparently liked it so much he posted it on his personal Facebook page.

http://y2u.be/Kav0FEhtLug

A MOUSE-EYE VIEW

Incredible hyper-slow-motion footage of a swooping owl

There are some things that bear endless re-viewing in slow-motion: the Zapruder JFK footage, Geoff Hurst's 1966 over-the-line goal or *that* Sharon Stone clip. This superb piece of wildlife footage can certainly join the list. It's an astonishing video in slow motion of a Eurasian Eagle Owl swooping to almost attack the camera lens. Filmed at a thousand frames a second, it reveals just how the bird moves its wings and controls its landing, giving a clear rendering of every individual feather as the owl positions itself to land.

http://y2u.be/SAz1L8DlvBM

HAVING A WHALE OF A TIME

See and believe – the whale they blew up!

Who would have thought that a 40-year-old grainy news story of a beached whale would attract over three million views? The story centres around a dead whale lying on the Oregon coastline back in 1970. When the locals got over the novelty, they started to notice the smell and demanded something be done. Fifty-odd sticks of dynamite later, we see the majestic mammal detonated and, as the reporter says, "The blast blasted blubber beyond all believable bounds." There are now T-shirts, a song, a website and, you never know, maybe a West End musical, commemorating the event.

http://y2u.be/1_t44siFyb4

WELCOME TO HAMSTER-JAM

The rise and rise of the gangsta hamsters

What's the best way to advertise a trendy compact car aimed at young women? If you said hip hop hamsters, go straight to your nearest ad agency and demand yourself a job. The gold-chained, headphone-wearing, hoodied-up dancing hamsters have driven right over the opposition in ads that saw them eschew the traditional stationary wheel for a set of cool Kia Soul wheels. With over 20 million views, this is the most successful in the series, but if you like the shuffling, rapping rodents, there's minutes more entertainment just waiting for you.

http://y2u.be/4zJWA3Vo6TU

RUMBLE IN THE OUTBACK

Who'd win a fight between an emu and a kangaroo?

This farmyard tussle actually pits two of Australia's favourite creatures against each other. Well, you know what those emus are like after a few too many acacia leaves on a Friday night. And, a little like the scene outside your local kebab house of a weekend, there's a lot of posturing and posing, but not a lot in the way of knock-out blows. If you listen carefully, you can even catch one of the emus screaming, "Leave him, Shane, he's not worth it!"

http://y2u.be/d9OBqYbZ99c

LOSING IT BIG TIME

The strange story of the angry German kid

We've all been frustrated by video games. You're on the verge of reaching the next level and bang goes your last life or they put a ridiculous challenge in that you are never going to solve in a million years — but this lad has gone ballistic and the game hasn't even started yet. OK, watch it now before you read the next bit. In 2006 the post went viral, spawning numerous parodies and tributes, but a few years later it emerged that the whole thing was staged. Do you believe that confession? Many remain convinced this is the real "losing it" deal.

http://y2u.be/q8SWMAQYQf0

YES SIR, I CAN BOOGIE

From Elvis to Jay-Z in seven minutes

It took a thirtysomething, bald, white guy to nail the ultimate YouTube dance video. Judson Laipply's witty, energetic and imaginative sketch called *The Evolution of Dance* was at one time YouTube's most watched and top-rated video. Judson twists, body pops, robots, breakdances and headbangs his way through over 30 songs in a six-minute routine that has racked up over 200 million views. It's entertaining enough, but you might feel it's better performed by a real robot! In which case, check out *Evolution of Dance* by NAO Robot and see for yourself.

http://y2u.be/dMH0bHeiRNg

DOGGY STYLE

An exercise video with a difference – a big difference

There's some really odd stuff on YouTube. Yes, really. It's not uncommon to stumble across somewhat strange, nay bizarre, videos, but this one is just right out there, way past weird – and it's somehow important to share it. It's called *Poodle Exercise with Humans*. We are told that it's a word-for-word parody of a workout video by US celebrity Susan Powter and was made by Japanese pop artist Nagi Noda. However, there's nothing to warn us that it's completely bonkers, totally mesmerizing and could well lead to some disturbing, not to say surreal, nightmares.

http://y2u.be/g8hsl6Y2L-U

"WHAT? YOU ATE ALL THE MEAT IN THE FRIDGE!"

The ultimate dog tease

"What's up, Rover?"

"It's all cat, cat, cat, isn't it? Haven't they got anything for dogs on YouTube?"

"Well, what about this? It stars a gullible German shepherd dog named Clarke."

"That's great. Click it!"

"It was the big hit in 2011. And Clarke talks – just like you!"

"Yes! That code now, please!"

"You sure? It's all about how his owner ate all the meat in the fridge."

"What!!!"

http://y2u.be/nGeKSiCQkPw

DROP AND ROLL

Rally driver in dramatic cliff-side plunge

This one's for the crash voyeurs, but it's OK – amazingly no one gets hurt. This is from the Race to the Clouds, the annual race that climbs 1,542m (5,000ft) to the summit of Pikes Peak in Colorado. Some vehicles don't make it that far and that was the fate of rally driver Jeremy Foley and his co-driver as they lost control on a bend, rolling over 14 times as they plunged 30m (100ft) down a 45-degree slope into a rock field. For a shorter but just as impressive in-car view of the incident, look at *Jeremy Foley Pikes Peak Crash in Car Video #1*. Rallytastic!

http://y2u.be/JDVLo08vTXY

TAKING A DIVE

Going for the sympathy vote

This is a great clip because it gets to the root of human behaviour. ATTENTION — I WANT ATTENTION AND I WANT IT NOW! Some of us continue to audition for TV talent shows, but most learn to hold it in. Now this little fella is determined to get some TLC and is going about it in the only way he knows — crying for sympathy. And if that doesn't work, he's going to try Plan B, which is, er ... more crying for sympathy. The only trouble is, he's been to the Cristiano Ronaldo School of Soccer Diving — and he's kidding no one.

http://y2u.be/_XObo46us_A

MONKEY BUSINESS

This classic animal advert is top banana

Back in the days before YouTube, animals who could talk like humans – and this will amaze many of you – were actually very rare, and most people could get their fix only via the adverts that interrupted the evening's viewing on their newly purchased colour TV sets. If the internet had existed in 1971, this clip would have gone super-viral. It shows that you can still find the old gems online – and stands up to the best that YouTube can offer.

http://y2u.be/HgzEBLa3PPk

IN THE DOGHOUSE

Someone's helped themselves to the Kitty Cat treats...

This is quite possibly the best whodunit on the web. We have incontrovertible evidence found at the crime scene, two suspects and a detective determined to get to the bottom of the matter. But who will crack first? Is there a tell-tale sign that reveals the perpetrator of the heinous crime? Will the guilty party give themselves away? And when the verdict is delivered, will they accept their punishment without complaint? The famous Denver the Guilty Dog is worth every one of its 25 million views!

http://y2u.be/B8ISzf2pryl

A WHOLE NEW BALL GAME

The magical art of contact juggling

Contact juggling: it's a kind of cross between a magic trick, the boring juggling you see on variety shows and a martial art — and it's pretty cool. This clip, in which a small crystal ball appears to be floating in mid air with the "juggler" merely caressing and rolling the ball in order to manipulate it, is a fabulous example of the supposedly ancient art. The mystical-looking sphere is called a fushigi ball, but the magic is all in the hands. Check out the *Fushigi Ball Explained* clip if you want to see how it's done.

http://y2u.be/mbMDI-JSb30

OK, BUT WHERE'S MY BURRITOS?

Mexican music meets Arctic whale in Connecticut

One can't help thinking that surreal artist Salvador Dalí would have absolutely loved YouTube – unfortunately he died in 1989, a full 16 years before the first post. Where else, apart from Dalí and his friends' work, would you find a mariachi band serenading a Beluga whale? It's not as if Juno from the Marine Life Aquarium in Connecticut can actually hear through the glass and the water, although, to be fair, she does seem to be enjoying and nodding along to the performance – and at least she didn't have to put any money in the hat to get them to move along.

http://y2u.be/ZS_6-lwMPjM

THE HERO HOG

Pig saves baby goat – or does it?

It was earth-shattering. Like the day you found out that Father Christmas wasn't real. This video, which was uploaded to YouTube in September 2012, went viral in hours. It was like a message from above. Everything on Earth is just fine. If a pig can rescue a baby goat, then one day surely we can all live in harmony? Just five months later the sickening truth was out: the whole thing was staged. It was revealed to have taken a 20-person crew, including animal trainers and scuba divers, to arrange the "stunt". And they wonder why we are all such cynics!

http://y2u.be/g7WjrvG1GMk

GOING NOWHERE – SLOWLY

A classic drunken escalator fail

Real life throws up stuff that is so much funnier than any comedy show. This two-minute clip of late-night life in a London Underground station is simply hilarious. It stars one very drunk Japanese businessman attempting to walk down an up escalator and a kind young woman who desperately tries to point him in the right direction. There's something about the man's steadfast plodding despite his lack of progress and the woman's frustrated but determined refusal to let him keep going all night that brings a smile to your face and a warmth to your cockles.

http://y2u.be/txNmh8i3AyA

DANGEROUS CYCLE-PATH

The New York bike lane vigilante

When the New York police gave Casey Neistat a ticket, fining him for not riding his bike in the cycle lane, they picked on the wrong guy. Casey was already a YouTube star, having produced an iPod battery warning campaign and other popular movies. So, taking the fine to heart, Casey decides to try sticking to the bike lane as instructed and filming the result. He's making a serious point about the obstacles in his way, but it makes for amusing if painful viewing. If you like this, try Casey's equally witty *Make It Count*.

http://y2u.be/bzE-IMaegzQ

LEAVE CHRIS ALONE

A heartfelt defence of Britney Spears

Nobody likes a bully, but too few of us are prepared to stand up to them. Chris Crocker is different. In 2008 he uploaded a video of himself speaking in defence of someone he knew named Britney. Apparently all kinds of bad things were being said about this young woman and Chris was not prepared to put up with it any more. Well, years later we don't know whether the inexcusably hurtful things hurled at Britney have stopped, but we do now know that some pretty terrible things have been said about Chris himself. Enjoy the tear-interrupted, over-hysterical, ridiculously camp rant— but please, leave Chris alone!

http://y2u.be/kHmvkRoEowc

DOG TREAT

Bizzle Gets Some Dunkers – great title, great video

Who has had more YouTube views: the cute, mischievous cat or the faithful lovable dog? The cat vs dog battle is hard fought, so the success of this video led to an appeal from the cat lovers. How can it count as a dog video when the American bulldog clearly has human arms and hands? What kind of monstrous creature is this anyway? From these few minutes it appears pretty benign and content to sit at the dinner table and munch its way through a snack. Another five million to the canines, though? You decide.

http://y2u.be/bgoDkwwpFx0

TECHNOLOGICAL GENIUS

Brief but brilliant YouTube gag

Afraid of Technology is the best short on YouTube. A video version
of a one-liner, it's a perfectly set up gag that's over and done with
in five seconds (which is not to say you won't be repeating
it over and over again). There is a definite art to framing the
joke in such a short time, so for some more examples have
a look at: *Drunk Old Man Stopped and Breath Tested by
Police*, *Pretty Much Everywhere It's Gonna be Hot* and the
inspired *Hercules – DISAPPOINTED*.

http://y2u.be/Fc1P-AEaEp8

THINKING INSIDE THE BOX

Meet the World Wide Web's most famous cat

This video features Maru, a Scottish Fold cat who lives in Japan. Now Maru likes boxes — big boxes, small boxes, slim boxes, tiny boxes. Indeed he loves boxes and that, along with his general cat-ness, is Maru's talent. However, as was nearly once said, there's something about Maru, and his 300-film YouTube channel has over 300,000 subscribers and his videos have been viewed more than 100 million times. Even if you don't like cats, watch this one through because it has a nice, funny ending.

http://y2u.be/2XID_W4neJo

SOMETHING THE CAT BROUGHT IN

Introducing Nora the piano cat

We've kept the cat quota as low as possible, but there's really no avoiding this. As amazing videos go, *Nora: Practice Makes Purr-fect* is right up there (better than *Keyboard Cat* anyhow). Agreed, any old mog can plink plonk along the piano and get some sound out of it, but this cat does truly seem to have some musical talent. The clip features her hard at work composing and playing a duet with (presumably) a human partner. Of course, Mozart was writing a concerto at the age of five, but then he couldn't bring up furballs and lick his own...

http://y2u.be/TZ860P4iTaM

EVERYBODY FREEZE!

The great Grand Central freeze

The Freeze is a well-tried flash mob performance, but it took New York's Improv Everywhere (mentioned elsewhere in these pages) to really pull it off in style. This one involved over 200 "IE Agents" gathering in the main concourse of New York City's iconic Grand Central Station. As travellers bustled through the busy railway station, the agents mingled among them. Suddenly, at the agreed time, they froze in their pose. They then held still for five minutes, while stunned commuters and tourists either joined in or stood wondering just what the hell was going on.

http://y2u.be/jwMj3PJDxuo

SPINE CHILLER

The ultimate dare

We'd say don't try this at home, but, honestly, who would be so stupid? The Children of Poseidon are three blokes from Perth who make some of the most eye-watering videos on YouTube. Having tried setting each other on fire, launching themselves from shopping trollies, eating cat food and supergluing their lips shut, they were still searching for that elusive internet hit. Then they came up with *Cactus Bodyslam*, in which Jeffabel Poseidon hurls himself semi-naked at a large spiny cactus plant. It is painful to watch, agonizing for the Aussie idiot, but it did the trick.

http://y2u.be/PHSJCMkUa9Y

PISTOL PARENTING

Teenager's dad dishes out some tough love

If you want to cause an internet rumpus, try taking on the
teenage psyche. An American parent called Tommy Jordan
became exasperated with his 15-year-old daughter Hannah after
she had posted a letter on her Facebook profile, criticizing him
and her mother. His response was unusual, to say the least.
He recorded his own, alarming but hilarious, message and posted
it on her Facebook wall. When that was uploaded to YouTube,
the whole teenage world had a hissy fit on Hannah's behalf,
while parents stood shoulder-to-shoulder with their new
hero. Are you ready to join the fracas?

http://y2u.be/kl1ujzRidmU

FRUIT SHOOT

Bringing a phone game to life

Fruit Ninja is one of the most popular smart phone games ever. It's a simple affair in which you slash fruit in half with a samurai sword, but it has proved as addictive as sugar. So what better wheeze than to play the game for real? Out in the woods someone throws some fruit at a guy in fancy dress and he dices and slices his way through them. Try it next time you fancy a fruit salad – it's not as easy as they make it look – but it is a whole lot of fun.

http://y2u.be/w-IIZmPPNwU

SELF ANALYSIS

What would you ask your pre-teenage self?

Jeremiah McDonald, age 12, is clever, charismatic and funny, and he also had considerable insight. Jeremiah McDonald, age 32, is also pretty smart and knows how to put a film together. And guess what? They're one and the same person! This six-minute YouTube gem was 20 years in the making, because, by means of an old VHS he made in 1992, Jeremiah has fashioned a dialogue with his young self. It works incredibly well, succeeding in being touching, funny and thought-provoking at the same time.

http://y2u.be/XFGAQrEUaeU

TOTALLY SPACED OUT

Cool experiments from outer space

You never know when you might need to wring out a wet towel in space, so this clip of a simple experiment, made by the International Space Station, could prove invaluable. Astronaut Chris Hadfield takes a compressed puck of official NASA-issue towel, squirts water over it and then wrings it out. It might sound dull, but the effect is totally cool. When you see the amazing way that water responds to zero gravity, you'll be transfixed. Budding space cadets might want to investigate more brilliant ISS videos, such as *Clipping Fingernails in Space* and *Cooking Spinach in Space*.

http://y2u.be/IMtXfwk7PXg

THIS'LL QUACK YOU UP

Cat and duck in *Jaws* remake

Sometimes the response to a viral YouTube video should just be "Why?" As in "Why on God's Earth would someone dress a cat up in a shark costume, put them on a Roomba [one of those robotic flat vacuum cleaners] and let them chase a duck around the room?" But watch this video and none of these questions will matter, because you'll just be so pleased that they bothered. And do watch all the way through — you don't want to miss the dog!

http://y2u.be/Of2HU3LGdbo

SO COOL

Are you ready to join the *Charlieissocoollike* bandwagon?

Charlie McDonnell has been posting videos on YouTube since he
was 16. He's now in his mid-20s and has become one of
the site's top celebrities. By posting simple, amusing blogs about
his life under the name *Charlieissocoollike*, his was the first
YouTube UK channel to reach one million subscribers. The
cute-looking, Bieber-esque Charlie then became a star in the
US when Oprah featured his *How to be English* video. This one
is typically *Charlieissocoollike* as he duets with himself in
his usual self-deprecating but instantly likeable way.

http://y2u.be/pVo-S9ns2_A

BEDTIME BANDIT

Kyle, the two-year-old toy thief

Kyle Moser isn't the first burglar to be caught in the act on video, but he might well be the first two-year-old. When Kyle's eight-year-old sister told her parents that her little brother was stealing things from her room at night, they told her to lock the door. She did as they suggested but still found her toys were going missing. Intrigued, the parents decided to secretly film what was happening and when Kyle ingeniously went on the hunt for a prized unicorn pillow pet, they were rewarded with a perfect 90-second crime caper.

http://y2u.be/8wk-qRfJQPM

WHO ARE YOU CALLING A ROBOT?

Eavesdropping on a conversation between talking robots

Chatbots are robots programmed to engage in human-type dialogue. They are becoming so sophisticated that they can sometimes fool people into thinking they are having a real conversation. So what happens if you put two of these bots up against each other? Will it be like one of those late-night TV arts debates? Or bons mots recalling the barbed wit of Dorothy Parker? Not wanting to give away any answers here, but listen out for the line "I am not a robot, I am a unicorn"!

http://y2u.be/WnzlbyTZsQY

CAN I HAVE MY POCKET MONEY NOW?

The sweetest duet on the web

When you think of father–daughter musical duets, names like Frank and Nancy Sinatra, Johnny and Rosanne Cash or maybe even Loudon and Martha Wainwright come to mind. But Jorge Narvaez and his daughter Alexa knock the spots off them all – because Alexa is only six years old and is as cute as a button. Their cover of "Home" by Edward Sharpe and the Magnetic Zeroes is enough to make even the most unsentimental of souls melt down and weep. What's more, it earned them 25 million views, was taken up for a Hyundai commercial and won them a place on *America's Got Talent*.

http://y2u.be/L64c5vT3NBw

READY, STEADY ... DONE?

How quickly can you link to this page?

It's a speedster's world and don't those YouTubers know it!
Think you're quick at something? Knitting? Slicing watermelon?
Texting? Take a quick search, and you'll find someone with
superhuman skills that put your efforts to shame. Alternatively,
spend five enjoyable minutes watching a compilation of
awesome talents – a collection of speedy stuff from the world's
fastest clapper to the snappiest Rubik cube solver and the
quickest undresser to a record-breaking pizza maker.
Just hope your broadband speed is up to it.

http://y2u.be/k4oCrCwEIEA

DOES MY ASS LOOK BIG IN THIS?

A clip that's outstanding in its field

YouTube has cornered the market in by-passer filming. Wherever there's someone in an embarrassing situation crying out for help, there's someone else ready to stop what they are doing – and film it. The poor chap in this clip has obviously been caught short while out in the country and decided to nip into a nearby field to answer nature's call. What he couldn't have suspected is that he would arouse the interests of an over-excited donkey – or that someone would get their mobile out as he yelled for assistance.

http://y2u.be/JPMZfxUeLvk

GETTING HIGH

Let these kids test your fear of heights

When we were kids we'd hang out in the park, maybe take in a movie or, if we were being really brave, explore the local derelict house. But these youngsters have other ideas. Their concept of a fun day out seems to be climbing out on the arm of a crane, hundreds of feet in the air. The clip is entitled *Your Hands WILL Sweat After Watching This!* and they're not wrong. It's a teeth-grindingly anxious watch, even when you've already seen it five times. And, if you suffer from vertigo, make sure you're sitting down when you try to watch.

http://y2u.be/tfZ1NyS6Mzw

A-MAZE-ING!

Is this the world's scariest game?

The Scary Maze Game is a YouTube phenomenon. You simply film your victim as they use their mouse to guide the cursor through an ever-more complex maze without touching the walls. On completion they are greeted with a close-up picture from the movie *The Exorcist*, along with an ear-piercing scream. Whether a hilarious prank or a mean-spirited waste of time, people persist in posting videos of their friends, family, social workers in embarrassing states of fright. Most are dull, but this is the exception – a truly, truly funny reaction.

http://y2u.be/469zNXTCHdk

WE WILL NOT LET YOU GO

When words fail you, try the lyrics of Queen

Across the world the fight for justice by those facing police charges takes many different forms. Some hire expensive lawyers to get them off the hook, others find protest groups are organized in their favour, and the less fortunate face a hard, lonely struggle. Watching this video it appears that defendants taking issue with the police in Canada can argue their case through the performance of classic pop hits. Here Robert Wilkinson, arrested for intoxication and finding mere words insufficient, resorts to Queen's "Bohemian Rhapsody" in an impassioned plea for his release.

http://y2u.be/fqymcJRSbxl

KEEP YOUR HAIR ON

The famous homemade wig prank

Prank time again. It's giving the game away a bit, but it doesn't diminish the feel-good effect of this video from Jozaeh in Australia. He came up with the inspired idea of shaving his hair off, collecting it all up and making a wig out of it. It looks pretty authentic, good enough not to be noticed by the friends and family he gets to pose with him, but of course the best part is the reveal. The wonderful, if surprised, reactions to his ingenious trick have already gleaned the video two-and-a-half million views.

http://y2u.be/ZmsP2s5euhk

YOUTUBE'S SENIOR MOMENT

The oldies are still the goodies

Old people, eh? Blinking hilarious. Well, at least these two old dears are. Introducing octogenarians Bruce and Esther Huffman from McMinnville in Oregon, USA. They became unlikely YouTube celebs when their granddaughter posted a three-minute clip of their attempt to snap a photograph on their new laptop computer. It's not just about laughing at senior citizens meeting technology (fun though that is), there's also some music as Bruce stretches his vocal cords, some romance, some light bawdy suggestiveness and plenty of slapstick. At one point Esther says, "I don't know what I'm recording." Comedy gold, madam, comedy gold.

http://y2u.be/FcN08Tg3PWw

A WALK ON THE WILD SIDE

Hey, Randall, tells us all about that crazy Honey Badger

Ever watched a wildlife show and thought just how boring the voiceover was? Struggling actor Randall thought just that and decided to record his own narration. What made some fairly boring footage of a badger go madly viral? Maybe his marvellously camp delivery? Perhaps his appalled reaction to mildly gross animal behaviour? But most probably the brilliant way he appears to make it all up as he watches the clip. It's great to think of David Attenborough watching in disbelief, thinking, "What, I didn't have to fight my way into the heart of those rainforests?"

http://y2u.be/4r7wHMg5Yjg

SOMETHING A LITTLE FISHY

From market stall to Number One

Muhammad Shahid Nazir's story is a YouTube rags to riches fairy tale. When Nazir found a job on a fish stall at Queen's Market in East London, his boss told him he had to shout to get customers' attention. Reluctant to just yell, Nazir preferred to sing his message about the cheap seafood on sale. When a customer uploaded a video of him singing, it went viral – soon spawning a music video complete with Bollywood dancers. The song hit the charts and, despite being banned in his home country of Pakistan, turned Nazir into a global star.

http://y2u.be/ETSI8gWsFZ0

THEY'RE HUMANS JIM, BUT NOT AS WE KNOW THEM

A superb collection of extreme stunts

We're a strange race, us humans. Most of us consider getting out of the armchair a major physical accomplishment and making a cup of coffee a feat of superb dexterity. Meanwhile, it seems there's another human race whose bravery, skills and co-ordination make us look like cack-handed apes from another planet. Put together by the British band Hadouken!, whose own rocking single provides the soundtrack to *People are Awesome 2013*, this is a video which rounds up a series of mind-blowing jumps, spins, somersaults and other incredible sporting feats. Yes, maybe you should have a rest now…

http://y2u.be/A6XUVjK9W4o

SCREAM IF YOU WANT TO GO FASTER

Ride the world's scariest rollercoasters

YouTube delights in re-creating the thrills of the world's best theme park rides. With footage captured from the actual seat, you get a pretty realistic rollercoaster trip in the comfort of your own home. However, to have a true simulation of the experience you are welcome to: queue outside the door for an hour, give all your cash to whoever's standing around looking bored and get someone to throw a bucket of water over you at appropriate points. Still, if you are going to be sick, at least you can use a bowl rather than the hood of the person in front.

http://y2u.be/QriRtKvLd2c

FOOTBALL FOCUS

All the action from the Binocular Soccer Cup Final

Soccer has long been searching for an alternative to penalty shoot-outs to decide tied matches. Well, what about this idea from Japan? *The Takeshi Katano Show* staged a soccer match where the players all wore binoculars that made things appear closer than they really were. You'll have to admit that, as a sport, what Binocular Soccer lacks in technical ability and goalmouth action it more than makes up for in slapstick and people-falling-over hilarity. Seriously folks, this could be the funniest clip on the whole of YouTube.

http://y2u.be/-rRK7vlBG8A

SPICING THINGS UP

That damn-fool Cinnamon Challenge

What's the dumbest craze to have ever hit YouTube? Well, the Cinnamon Challenge is certainly among the contenders. Search on those words and you'll find hundreds of would-be YouTube heroes coughing and spluttering. The challenge is simple: try to swallow a tablespoon of cinnamon in 60 seconds without any water. YouTube personality and comedienne Glozell has earned the most CC hits with this hilarious attempt – watch it and you'll quickly get the idea. However, best stick to strictly armchair viewing on this one as doctors have slapped a health warning on trying the stunt yourself.

http://y2u.be/Cyk7utV_D2I

WHEN GOOD MASCOTS GO BAD...

A compilation of sporting mascot mishaps

Who'd be a sports team's mascot? You are incarcerated in a sweat-inducing, dignity-stripping, lumbering costume for hours on end; treated with contempt by the real stars of the show; and quickly discarded by the fans when the real action starts. No wonder there seems to be a seething rage forever building under those comic features and wobbly outfits. Of course, what the punters really love is to see their mascots truly humiliated — falling flat on their grinning bug-eyed face or taking a punch from the only other poor sap in the stadium with a oversize foam-rubber head. Sit back and enjoy.

http://y2u.be/iFVAxwErYAU

THIS CAT IS DEEP, MAN

The adventures of Henri, le Chat Noir

Henri may not be the most famous or adorable cat on the web, but he's got to be the most pretentious. His musings are delivered in captivating French, helpfully subtitled for those us whose knowledge of the language doesn't go much beyond "croissant" and "s'il vous plaît". We are thus able to glean that Henri the black cat is a tortured creature, but before you call the Cat Protection League, their literature states that unfortunately they can't do much for moggies suffering from existential angst. Definitely one for intellectuals and beret-wearers.

http://y2u.be/0M7ibPk37_U

PARALLEL UNIVERSE

The world's worst attempt at parking

Perhaps it was just one of those nightmares where frustration, despair and humiliation seem on a never-ending loop. Could it really have taken this Belfast woman a full half-an-hour to park in a space large enough to leave a bus? Was there really a gaggle of incredibly irritating students watching, jeering and cheering her every — and there were many — attempts to reverse into the space? Did they really post it on YouTube where it went viral and attracted media interest around the world? Oh yes, yes and yes. And very funny it is too!

http://y2u.be/tf4TIWECZ30

THE BESTEST ... YUMMA!

She forgot the blueberries – or did she?

Recipe time. Take one shaky camera and an ordinary kitchen.
Now add a sweet child eager to make a sensible video on how to
make a fruit salad and leave to stand for 20 seconds. Then pour
in a younger sister, very excitable, not quite as sensible, but still
equally sweet. Mix the ingredients until fabulous comic moments
rise to the surface. Upload in the YouTube oven and leave to
go viral. Other versions, parodies and remixes are available,
but none tastes half as good as the original.

http://y2u.be/yqEeP1acj4Y

I GOT THOSE CAN'T PLAY THE GUITAR BLUES

He's a guitarist and he's mighty angry

First of all a warning – this video is full of swearing, but it's far too funny to leave out, so if you're easily offended or a minor mute your sound and watch it anyway. This is all you need to know: the Treeman hails from Liverpool. His attempts to play guitar have made him a global YouTube star, but for all the wrong reasons. The Treeman is known as "the angriest guitar player in the world", because when he gets something wrong, he loses it completely and takes out his anger on the nearest person and object – himself and his guitar!

http://y2u.be/Vms_6_TSQuc

YOU'RE ALL THE MEME

Their part in Hitler's *Downfall*

Every now and then YouTube will remake a video to death.
Such was the fate of the parodies of *Downfall*, the movie of
Hitler's last days, in which the subtitles were changed to suit
every kind of rant from Disney buying Marvel to sub-prime
mortgages. They were, and still can be, very witty. Run through
the list and you might find one that suits your own sporting
or political cause, but to pick one that sums up the meme
is easy. Here Herr Hitler's tirade concerns the *Downfall*
parodies getting out of hand on YouTube. Clever, eh!

http://y2u.be/ChEXf91j2pU

BABY BOOMER

You're familiar with Iron Man — now meet 'Iron Baby'

Parodies of the blockbuster movie *Iron Man* are a popular YouTube meme. He's been remade in cardboard, recast in Thailand and been hilariously "honested" (search for *Honest Trailers*), but this one — with that special "cute baby" ingredient — went way out viral. The two-year-old is fabulously suited-up for bad-guy action, but quite how his parents are going to fare when it's time for a bottom clean-up is anyone's guess. And the way he deals with those evil bunnies makes you fear for mum and dad's lives when they tell him it's time for bed.

http://y2u.be/GaaQwJAww6s

BATMAN LIVES!

Jeb Corliss – the Amazing Flying Man

Jeb's idea of fun is putting on a tiny bat suit and jumping off cliffs, mountains and tall buildings. The most famous BASE jumper in the world, Jeb Corliss has leapt from the Eiffel Tower and the Space Needle and is banned from going near the Empire State Building. Strapped with a camera, he has the most magnificent collection of YouTube videos as he glides through the air in speeds of around 120mph. *Grinding the Crack* is his exhilarating ride through a Swiss gorge but check out *Grounded* if you want to see what happens when it all goes – literally – belly up.

http://y2u.be/TWfph3iNC-k

WALK THIS WAY

The amazing Japanese synchronized walking show

Who would believe that watching people walking could be quite so side-splittingly hilarious, but this is among the most bizarre and, in a strange way, fantastic videos out there. You've heard of synchronized swimmers with their impressive underwater routines, but synchronized walking takes things to another level. At first you might think it's just a military-style marching show, but oh no – these guys have more in their artillery than strolling up and down – stick with it and you are in for a treat. I bet you'll soon be signing the petition to make it an Olympic sport.

http://y2u.be/E7cQtbMtODk

DAT WAZ AWESOME!

It's always a good idea to finish with some fireworks

If you are not keen on profanities or blasphemous language it
might be worth giving this one a miss, but you'll be forgoing 60
seconds of panic-stricken delight. Perhaps this works because
we've all been there – watching a situation get out of hand and
being unable to do anything but voice your fears in exclamations
and appeals to the Almighty – but as a YouTube video it is
completely perfect. It features an exciting incident, steady
camera work, fabulous commentary and perfect subtitles –
with the "Jesus!" counter as the icing on the cake!

http://y2u.be/NRItYDKSqpQ

A RIGHT CHARLIE

Possibly the most famous home video in the world

Charlie Bit My Finger – Again! is just a sweet, short film of
two boys which any family would cherish. Perhaps, in years to
come, the parents might retrieve it and shed a nostalgic tear or
embarrass the boys in front of their girlfriends, but in uploading
it for the English boys' relatives in the USA, their father
inadvertently launched the most-viewed non-professional music
video on YouTube. Just what the magic ingredient is – the baby's
knowing look, the almost old-fashioned English accent,
or the earnest remonstrations – is a matter for discussion,
but if you could bottle it, you'd never need to work again...

http://y2u.be/_OBlgSz8sSM